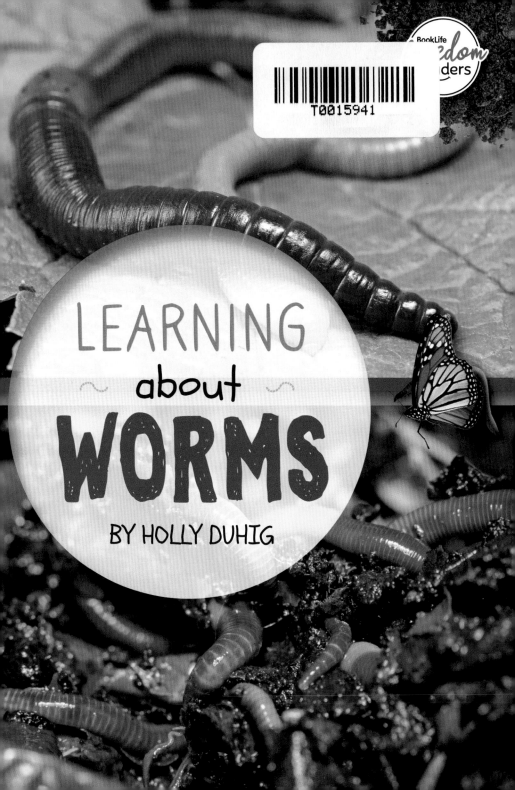

LEARNING
~ about ~
# WORMS

BY HOLLY DUHIG

BookLife
PUBLISHING

©2022
BookLife Publishing Ltd.
King's Lynn
Norfolk PE30 4LS

ISBN: 978-1-80155-140-3

All rights reserved.
Printed in Poland.

Written by:
Holly Duhig

Edited by:
Charlie Ogden

Designed by:
Danielle Webster-Jones

A catalogue record for this book
is available from the British Library

Photo Credits

CONTENTS

WHAT IS A WORM?

A worm is an animal with a long body but no legs or skeleton. They live in the ground.

Many worms like to live under the ground in damp soil. These worms are called earthworms. There are over 2,000 species of earthworm, and they live all over the world.

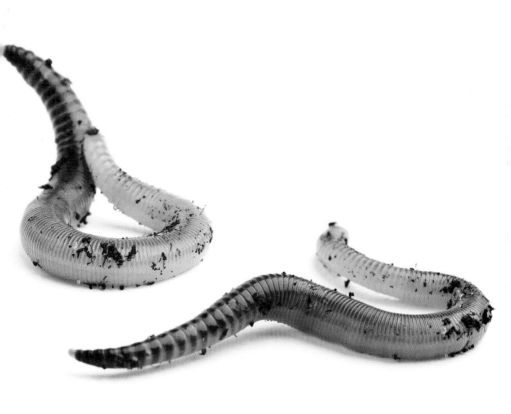

Earthworms usually grow seven to eight centimetres long. Their bodies are pink or brown and are made of many ring-like segments.

Worms have a thicker ring near their heads. This makes a slimy substance that helps them move.

HOW DO WORMS LAY EGGS?

Worms are neither male nor female so they can all lay eggs. When a worm lays an egg, it makes extra slime. This slime passes over the worm's body and covers the egg.

This slime forms a cocoon around the egg, which keeps
t safe. These cocoons are smaller than a grain of rice,
and each one can be home to 20 eggs.

WORM COCOONS

The cocoons usually take about three weeks to hatch.
However, if the weather is too cold or the soil is too dry,
the cocoons might stay unhatched for a lot longer.
This protects them from bad weather.

Worm cocoons can even survive being eaten by other animals. If eaten, they will come out in the animal's poo but will still be able to hatch.

WHERE DO WORMS LIVE?

Earthworms live in tunnels that they make in the soil. In the winter, they dig deeper underground where it is warmer.

Some people have a container in their garden for old food and dead plants that worms can live in. This is called a wormery.

WHAT DO WORMS EAT?

Worms are not fussy eaters. They will eat anything, from fruit and vegetables to dead plants and animals. They eat whatever they come across as they move along.

Worms do not have teeth, so they cannot chew food.
Instead, they eat small stones and grains of sand
which help to grind up food once it reaches
the worm's stomach.

WHAT DO WORMS DO?

Earthworms spend a lot of time looking for food. When it rains, worms come out of the ground. This is because the water helps them to move quicker, making it easier to find food.

Seagulls are known for hunting worms by tapping the ground with their feet to make it sound like it is raining. When a worm appears, the gull quickly grabs it with its beak.

HOW DO WORMS HELP?

In one acre of soil there might be as many as one million worms. Worms break down the nutrients in the food they eat. These nutrients come out in the worm's poo. Another name for worm poo is worm castings.

The nutrients in worm castings go back into the soil. This makes the soil more fertile, which means it is easier for plants to grow in it.

There are many species of worms in the world. If you have ever been to the beach, you might have seen small, squiggly piles of sand. These are left behind by lugworms which live under the sand on beaches.

Some worms live in the sea. The bootlace worm is the longest species of worm. The longest bootlace worm ever found was over 55 metres long.

FUN FACTS

Worms eat a lot. They eat half their body weight in food every day.

Some people take part in competitions to see who can get the most worms to come out of the ground. This is called worm charming.

QUESTIONS

1: **What do worms eat to help them grind up food?**
   a) Small stones and grains of sand
   b) Broccoli and spaghetti
   c) Paper and cardboard

2: **How long was the longest bootlace worm?**

3: **What are worm castings?**

4: **How do birds get worms to come out of the ground?**

5: **What would happen to plants if there were no worms?**